Baptized By Fire

A Lighting of the Soul

Joe Brazzle

ISBN: 1500107255
ISBN 13: 9781500107253

When the fog of suffering is lifted, the smallest ray of love will reflect the face of God.

I dedicate this book to all the warriors that have trusted me to guide them to a better place. May God smile on your adventures!
Godspeed, friends.

Why did I write this book?

On August 17, 2007, in Fort Bragg, North Carolina, I was emergency airlifted from demolitions Range #47 to the University of North Carolina's medical hospital for treatment. I had received severe trauma to the eyes, face, neck, and body, and I was placed in a coma for stabilization. No past experience had truly prepared me for the pain and agony I endured during those times. Although my military career had come to a close, an unexpected intimate relationship with God emerged. These amazing experiences forced me to write this essay.

I intend to identify the spiritual insights that emerged after my trauma. My prayer is that these words will find their homes in the hearts of any human being who has been at odds with his or her spirituality or purpose. I also pray that these chapters deliver a message of hope to those who have given up the fight for God. Most of all, I pray that my personal story of recovery is a testament to the grace and mercy of our divine creator.

Contents

Embrace the Challenge at: *www.baptizedbyfire.com*

one

Accept Yourself Entirely

In hindsight, I find it funny how I have spent so much of my life trying to become someone or something. It seems I have been constantly fighting to meet goals, benchmarks, and expectations of the world and people around me. There is no better place than the US Army to help me become *all that I can be* when it comes to the journey of becoming someone!

My first real spiritual insight as I recovered from my injuries was the duality of my human imperfection and the divine perfection that operates within me. I know what you are thinking "Wow, did he just go there?" Yes, I did! Let me explain: I first confronted my human imperfection during the following life experience.

Last Chance

Demo Range # 47, Fort Bragg, North Carolina

We must have been the only platoon in the battalion that was training on that Friday. I had argued with my commander for weeks about the intense pace of the training, but he insisted that we push the men. This was hard for me to accept because I had just finished my sixth deployment and knew of our company's extreme fatigue. In Afghanistan, we had suffered through more than our fair share of shit and needed some time to unravel and adjust. Unfortunately, I was also accustomed to supporting my commander's decisions, despite my better judgment.

August 17, 2007, was jam-packed with combat training. Breaching drills, field expendiant bangalores, and platoon-suppressive fire exercises were all crammed into the day. It was too hot to train at combat speed, but we were experts at playing the game to appease overzealous commanders, so we ran full throttle despite the risks. Little did I know that by close of business, playing the game would be an unforgettably poor choice for me and for several others. As the day came to a close, the noncommissioned officer in charge (NCOIC) had reported to the range officials that all explosions and gunfire had ceased. During our final inspection, we realized that live explosive residue still remained in tiny fragments all over the ground. A group of soldiers gathered around me and the

NCOIC to seek further guidance. "Fuck, Sergeant Brazz, what do we do with all this tiny C4?" asked a young soldier.

The NCOIC and I concurred that burning the residue would keep us from reopening the range and prevent any confusion about our earlier reports that the range could be closed. "Can you even burn this stuff?" one soldier inquired.

"Sure, this is how we got rid of our leftover demo down range. It neutralizes the explosive content without having to send the sound of an explosion for the entire enemy to hear," the NCOIC said.

The small group of soldiers dug a hole and began to burn the remaining explosive residue as directed. I rushed back and forth, searching for every tiny bit of C4 I could find. I fed piece after piece into the flames, hoping to finally put an end to an exhausting week. As I approached the fire once more, I was startled to see the NCOIC holding a full roll of detonation cord in his hand. He was moving forward to toss the roll in. "STOP, NO, don't throw..." Boom! The whole roll of detonation cord exploded like a supernova. I had just enough time to turn my body sideways before the explosive force assaulted my face and the flames engulfed my body. Hot shrapnel ripped through me; heat ran over every inch of my face, and I surrendered to the blast. I tried to pick myself up from the ground, but nothing would act as it should. My arms and legs felt detached, and strength was foreign to me. Never had I felt more afraid than at that very moment. I lay on the ground, waiting helplessly for someone to approach. I could only make out the NCOIC's voice in the distance. He screamed and screamed about the pain his face was in—screams that became etched in my memory forever.

I can recall the distant voices of soldiers reacting to the blast. "Don't worry, Sergeant Brazz, we're gonna get you out of here." By this time I knew that my situation was dire. A rush of warm blood began to infuse my body. I could feel numbness setting into my joints and muscles. I mustered together enough words to ask for forgiveness from our Lord and humbled myself to his mercy. As the high winds of the approaching helicopter swirled up the earth, I knew the fight for my life was coming to an end—at least my part was. Quickly, I searched for a reason that this happened, but found none. Frustrated by the absence of any organized thought, I was forced in that moment to confront my imperfections.

There are only two lessons in life...painful and expensive.
—*Rashe Hall, combat battle buddy*

I was truly unaware of our human imperfection until that moment in my life. I always thought that there was a way to train, learn, or practice my way to perfection. I had considered myself, as a combat engineer, to be among the best the US Army had to offer. I had attended nearly all of the training schools available for my job and even some others just to add flair. I was well decorated for service and revered among my peers. I was exceptionally good at training soldiers to face the realities of combat and even better at leading them through the horrors that come along with the ride. After ten years as a combat engineer, I had survived IEDs, mortars, firefights, and suicide bombers—all without a single scratch to highlight my future drunken bar stories.

My brief success in the military was enough to convince me that perfection could be obtained through diligent practice and discipline. I also believed that God was present in the world but not necessarily present in me. I had not trained, learned, or practiced hard enough to present myself to God and believed he would never approve of the thoughts, actions, and habits of my world. Man, did I have it wrong! This fragmented view caused an endless pursuit of perfection that I could never attain. Although it is in our nature to grow and get better, perfection is out of reach for our human hands. All of our noble attempts will fall shy of the mark. In my own pain, I was forced to accept my imperfections and willingly conceded any hope of divine intervention over to God.

> *The consciousness of one's inner value is anchored in higher, more spiritual things, and cannot be shaken.*
> —Viktor E. Frankl

When I was forced to concede to the providence of God, I was truly prepared to stand before him on my next breath. Fortunately, I returned to consciousness several days later and was filled with the excitement of life. I was eager to get well and enjoy life because I would never worry about perfection again.

Still Here

Burn Ward, University of North Carolina– Chapel Hill, North Carolina

I'd been awake for several hours listening to the little girl down the hall scream in agony about the burns on her body. Although I was unable to help, I prayed over and over for someone to give her something that would help with the pain. I could hear the nurses encouraging her to move around, but she just shouted, "NO, I CAN'T," wailing, "IT HURTS SO BAD!" It seemed the pain had gotten the best of her. The ward nurses seemed insistent that she move around to keep her burns free of infection and bed rot. Finally, after bouts of crying and compromise, the child was soothed, and the ward returned to the beeps of hospital equipment and whispering nursing staff.

I remember surveying my body in awe for the first time after the explosion. I glanced down at the bandages that covered my arm and leg. I had yet to really inspect my physical state until that night. I could move most parts well, but the numbness of the morphine ran deep to the bone. I peeled back the bandage on my left arm back to reveal a grapefruit-sized hole in my bicep. I noticed plastic wrap around my left leg. I could watch the blood run through tubes on the vacuum-sealed wrap into a container. I couldn't believe my reality. Why did God spare me? I was certain that my life had ended on Range 47 and I came to terms with my imperfections. I recall lying on that hospital bed in the early morning hours and feeling completely overwhelmed by the love of God. God's divine presence wasn't outside somewhere waiting to be found. It lay at the core of my being—there to comfort me if I chose to look inside. There I sat, burns and all, with no control over my physical situation but absolutely clear about my spiritual situation. That morning I became aware of the relationship between my mind, body, and spirit. I realized how my imperfect body is led by my imperfect mind, all to cultivate my perfect spirit. That was the last day I ever denied the perfection of me. As God's creation, there is perfection to my life outside of my control.

> *The spirit of God dwells in you.*
> —Alice Brazzle, my sister

We are not condemned for who we are. This understanding can only come through accepting the imperfections of our flesh and the divine perfection of our spirituality. We cannot reach perfection because that which is perfection is not of our doing. It can neither be improved nor worked on. It can only be understood. The life force that is worth the life of Christ is not the imperfect, sinful, fleshly you but the spirit of God that lives in you. God's perfection is breathing through us and is only limited by the boundaries of our flesh. When we listen closely to the sounds from within, we can hear and be comforted by this perfection. This duality is working

every day and will continue to play a part in all that
we do.

> *This is the very perfection of a man, to*
> *find out his own imperfections.*
> —*Saint Augustine*

Actions On

Read:

❖ "Let anyone of you who is without sin be the first to throw a stone at her." —John 8:7 (NIV)

❖ For it is from within out of a person's heart, that evil thoughts come..." —Mark 7:21 (NIV)

❖ If we claim to be without sin, we deceive ourselves and the truth is not in us. —1 John 1:8 (NIV)

❖ Therefore there is now no condemnation for those who are in Christ Jesus, because through Christ Jesus the law of the Spirit who gives life has set you free from the law of sin and death. —Rom. 8:1–2 (NIV)

Pray:

Father, please help me release any ambitions for perfection, beliefs toward false idols, and worldly ways. Please help me accept my body and mind as they are. Help me align my mind and my body with my spirit. Guide my imperfect thoughts and actions to express your divine perfection in me.

Meditate:

Meditate on the follow scripture:

❖ Do not conform to the pattern of this world, but be transformed by the renewing of your mind. Then you will be able to test and approve what God's will is—his good, pleasing and perfect will. —Rom 12:2 (NIV)

Joe's Journal Points

1: I will own my shortcomings today. For they, also, are a part of me.

2: Things that we can't mend, heal, or put back together, we throw away. Today I am grateful for wounds that have healed, souls that have mended, and the lives that have been put back together!

3: Can we find contentment in the struggle?

4: Can I get comfortable with God's perfect design of my imperfection?

5: Is there a difficulty in my life that I have the power to influence?

6: Can I see my failure as an invitation to try again?

7: *Sunshine all the time, without rain, makes a desert.*
—*Arab proverb*

Reflection Reading

The first and best victory is to conquer self; to be conquered by self is, of all things, the most shameful and vile.
—*Plato*

two

Forgive Yourself and Others

Somewhere along my journey, I created a subtle habit of storing fear, shame, guilt, and anger from past experiences. I am not sure if this was something I overlooked as a young boy or even a young soldier, but it never seemed to be a big deal. I thought I confronted fear like any other man—with as much courage as one can muster. But when did I start to harbor these other feelings of shame, guilt, and mostly anger? It might have started back in Afghanistan when I experienced my first improvised explosive device (IED), which is a great bar story, by the way. Or maybe as far back as Bosnia when two Serbian fighter jets were in route to bomb my outpost. Whenever I acquired this habit, it certainly became quite a lot to handle after I was injured. Plagued with lucid flashbacks and many sleepless nights, I needed divine help with the pain that was rapidly growing in the pit of my stomach. Amazingly, the help that came to me was the notion to simply forgive myself and others. This was not an easy thing to accomplish because my torment seemed to be an assortment of difficult situations or events cast over a lifetime. Please permit me to share an experience that may shed some light about the power of forgiveness.

Too Heavy to Carry

Walmart Parking Lot

Although it was highly recommended that I not drive myself anywhere, on this day I really needed to get out. Several months after the accident, I drove a ways down the road and decided to pull into the back of Walmart's large parking lot. My daily dose of prescription drugs and the truck's movements had made me a little dizzy, so I reclined my seat and began to reflect. I thought about the several months that had dragged by and the hole in my heart that kept getting larger and deeper by the day. I also thought about God and his infinite plan. Why did this happen to me? Why take me through all those sticky times in combat just to have me cash it all in on a training range? I had so much anger harbored inside me that I could feel it running back and forth like hot water in my chest, arms, and legs. It had consumed every part of my being so that no part of me could embrace anything else. I recalled going through the motions with my family and friends that past Thanksgiving. Just to get through the holiday festivities, I pretended that I was shooting a holiday commercial for the US Army, and I was being ordered by some overcaffeinated director to smile and be happy. I also isolated myself from my family. I would stay up all night watching military history shows and pop my prescription medication. When it was time for my daughter to go to school or when everyone got home, I could be found unwashed and unconscious, deep beneath the pile of blankets on the living room couch. Through this period of denial and avoidance, something began to grow in the pit of my gut. The very thought of my injuries would unravel into an outburst of loud, obnoxious rants that were hurtful to any bystander willing to hang around. These dark days were so opposite of who I knew myself to be. Up to that point in my life, I couldn't recall ever really believing that any person was responsible for my circumstances. Consequently, those dark feelings became too heavy to hold on my own and began to fall square on the shoulders of the man who threw the detonation cord on Range 47. I became convinced that he was the source of all my pain.

Sitting in the back of that large parking lot, the anger became so overwhelming that I burst into tears and screamed out my frustrations. "God...are you fucking kidding me? A military killing machine, reduced to a helpless lump of shit? Tell me what leader gets hurt in a training accident." Sitting with my head in my hands, I watched rivers of tears run down the steering wheel of my pickup. My body shook and trembled with what felt like a lifetime of stored-up fear, shame, guilt, and anger. I wrapped both hands around my painful stomach and slowly rocked back and forth, whispering, "Show me mercy, please, mercy, show me mercy." Several moments later, the energy of the outburst began to fade and something shifted inside of me. God heard my cry and embraced me with his mercy. A voice in my head whispered, *Forgive and you will be forgiven.* Out of nowhere, feelings of compassion and acceptance rushed through my body. I had lightning bolt thoughts of my remaining health, my supportive wife, and of my loving son and daughter. I realized on that day that my situation was just like all my past situations: a product of how I chose to see it. My anger was fueling my decisions and changing my outlook on the external world. I no longer wanted to carry around the bag of anger and frustration that was polluting my life. I knew exactly what I needed to do. Quickly, I opened my phone and called the NCOIC. Not sure exactly what I would accomplish, I just knew it had to be done. As the phone rang, my heart began to race. When I heard his voice say, "Hello," I knew at that very moment why forgiveness is said to be an act for the self and not for others. He had no idea of my personal struggles with anger and rage. Nor did he know that I had volunteered him to be the scapegoat for my situation. Seconds into our conversation, I realized he was in the same boat as me—dealing with the shit of recovery. And the recovery life was hard enough. No one needed to add anything extra (like anger or rage) to the process. There were already psychotherapy, physical therapy, doctor appointments, drugs, sick days, pain days, numb days, and, on occasion, good days. So there in the parking lot of Walmart, I chatted with him about recovery, family, pain, and our overall well-being. My anger was immediately gone, and I was full of love and contentment. God's mercy and grace were sufficient for me.

When I held all my fear, shame, and guilt inside, I was constantly carrying the pain of this world in the pit of my stomach. That soon began to eat away at my mind, body, and spirit. Grace and self-forgiveness were the only options for me. I needed the kind of grace that only God could extend. Grace is defined as an underserved or unmerited kindness. It is this underserving grace that I extended to myself. Then and only then was I able extend the same to someone else. Now is a great time to point out that the extension of grace does not need to be a formal process. All that is needed is the internal awareness of releasing someone or something from the pit of your stomach through genuine forgiveness. This awareness ultimately set me free from harbored feelings of pain, resentment, anger, fear, shame, and guilt. Once the pain from my stomach had vanished, I could mourn for what I had lost and take inventory of what was still available.

> *Darkness cannot drive out darkness; only light can do that. Hate cannot drive out hate; only love can do that.*
> —*Martin Luther King Jr.*

Mourn and Take Inventory

If I am completely honest, I must admit I thought of countless ways not to write on this specific topic in this book but, fortunately, found no good reason to abandon it. I consider this an uncomfortable topic because in order to grow through pain, mourning must occur. But it is so damn _ugly_ and _unpredictable!_ I had struggled personally with a very dark and numbing process that lasted a little over two years. (I was surely not putting my best foot forward, to say the least). More importantly, I have either listened to or borne witness to hundreds of wounded warriors demonstrating the many diverse and creative rituals of mourning. Some may isolate away from friends, while others may become overly responsible and goal crazed. Some may sink into a very dark place of numbness, while others may explode in bouts of screaming and yelling. There are a lot of ways to express mourning, but the key point is that it needs to happen.

> _Blessed are they that mourn: for_
> _they shall be comforted._
> —_Matthew 5:4 (KJV)_

What Now, Smart Guy?

Phone Call from Tom, Early Morning
One Thursday afternoon my phone rang with the sad voice of a mourning soldier named Tom.

Tom's call was completely out of the blue. He was one of my soldiers from my platoon sergeant days. I could hear him faintly weeping, and his voice crackled over the phone. Tom had called to confess that his life was not what Uncle Sam had expected of him. He had been unable to mask the pains from *down range* and had begun to use drugs heavily. He was mourning and needed to share his pain. He started the call with, "Brazz...I need to talk to you." I could barely make out his words. "I, um...I, um...made such a mess of myself. I've disgraced my country and been overrun by fuckin' drugs! I don't think I can turn this thing around." After listening to his impromptu personal confession, I was at a loss for words. I wasn't sure if he really could turn his life around, but I was sure that he needed to forgive himself and allow the mourning process to begin. His mourning was painful and ugly but a necessary step to get through the storm. He had come to reality, and he was aware of all that lay before him. He saw the way ahead; he only needed to take inventory of the resources that were available within himself.

"Dem Dirty Boys! Ain't shit free!"
—*Bo McCalister, combat battle buddy and close friend*

Over the past several years, I have spent most of my days listening to the pains of veterans as a combat stress mentor with the Wounded Warrior Project. As I listened to each individual story of loss and struggle, I soon became aware of a common theme.

They all contained a period of mourning and of taking self-inventory. Some stories depicted dark places to cope with personal loss, while other stories detailed violent outbursts of rage to deal with anger. Some stories highlighted the hills and valleys of depression, while others skimmed the surface of addiction and attachment.

I will admit that I don't know much about the duration of mourning or even the intensity that one should express. All I can say is that it must happen in some form or another. Mourning is the process of accepting what or whom is lost. After this acceptance, we can began to embrace gratitude for what is remaining. This gratitude can increase when we take inventory.

> *If you know the enemy and know yourself, you*
> *need not fear the result of a hundred battles*
> —Sun Tzu

Actions On

Read:

❖ "My grace is sufficient for you, for my power is made perfect in weakness." —2 Cor. 12:9 (NIV)

❖ "Forgive and you will be forgiven." —Luke 6:37 (NIV)

Pray:

Father, allow me to accept your grace and mercy for myself. Through your mercy I forgive those who have hurt, wronged, or trespassed against me. Release me from the bondage of anger, hate, frustration, sadness, and fear.

Meditate:

Meditate on the following scripture:

I know what it is to be in need, and I know what it is to have plenty. I have learned the secret of being content in any and every situation, whether well fed or hungry, whether living in plenty or in want. —Phil. 4:12 (NIV)

Joe's Journal Points

1: If God has created everything and thus is everything, how can I be nothing?

2: The weak can never forgive. Forgiveness is the attribute of the strong. —Mahatma Gandhi

3: I am grateful to find understanding in the sweet joy of our inheritance.

4: Today I realized that I have carried "it" around for far too long!

5: I am now ready to let go of...

6: About 1.5 ounces of forgiveness should help finish this day. Two cups of gratitude should help start tomorrow. *Old recipes stay around for a reason!*

7: Let go and let God!

Reflective Reading

To live is to suffer—to survive is to find meaning in the suffering. If there is a purpose in life at all, there must be a purpose in suffering and in dying. But no man can tell another what this purpose is. Each must find out for himself and must accept the responsibility that his answer prescribes. If he succeeds he will continue to grow in spite of all indignities.

—Preface to Man's Search for Meaning

three

Follow a Reactionary Spirit

(Allow Christ to dwell in me)

I define following a reactionary spirit as the discipline to patiently wait and react to the guidance of God in the unfolding present moment. When I allowed the broom of forgiveness to tidy up my inner spirit, it cleaned out the worries, self-doubts, excuses, and resentments that were filling me with negativity. With my newfound space open and clean I asked God to live from within the depths of my heart. Through my daily practice of reading God's word, prayer, and meditation, I began to commune with God on a true spiritual level. With these daily practices becoming more of a habit, God's love began to consume my body and outer surroundings. Positive thoughts and energy began to make coincidences feel more like synchronicities, and the universe began to feel closer. In this discipline I have tried to remain open to the subtle signs and nuances of the profound happenings of life. These great moments have connected with other great moments, and a divine path of health, happiness, and fun has unfolded.

A Committed Enemy

Local Bar, Fort Bragg, North Carolina

I was sitting at the bar with a few close friends, and a deep discussion arose about the war in Afghanistan. We had all served there together and were wondering if any of our military efforts would really break the Taliban. I remained silent through the volley, watching my buddies recall several successful military offensives and the number of Taliban fighters killed (obviously exaggerated because of beer). Suddenly the conversation began to shift toward the Taliban's commitment to harassing our US forces and toward what the end game really was. I was eventually ask to contribute. "Brazz, you did three tours, surely you have something to say." I had been in hundreds of similar discussions before (especially in bars), but this time I was speechless. In trying to add value to the conversation, I became lost in my thoughts about the extreme commitment the Afghanis displayed around God. I recalled how often they prayed and structured their lives around their beliefs. I regretfully recalled a suicide bomber exploding into pieces before my very eyes because of his beliefs. Although I do not subscribe to their ways and methods, their commitment to God was far stronger than mine was. Struggling to add value to the conversation, I could only reply, "They are a committed bunch."

Leaving the bar that evening, I pondered over the Afghanis' religious motivations. What power could be so strong that a man would strap explosives to his chest and die for it? I had spent twenty-eight months fighting against their extreme religious beliefs but could not stand strong on the values of my own. I felt very sad and ashamed. That evening when I returned home, I vowed to start practicing my father's and mother's faith through prayer and devotional reading.

> *Somewhere a True Believer is training to kill you—*
> *This True Believer is not concerned about "how*
> *hard it is"; he knows either he wins or dies. He*
> *doesn't go home at 1700, he is home...He only*
> *knows the cause, now who wants to quit?*
> —*NousDefionsDoc*

Devotional Reading

> *Do not think that I have come to abol-*
> *ish the Law of the Prophets: I have not come*
> *to abolish them but to fulfill them.*
> —*Matt. 5:17 (NIV)*

Several years ago, my wife and I were in search of a church to attend for our growing family. During one

Easter holiday we decided to attended a small christian church which was right around the corner from our house. As we walk up to the entrance we were greeted by a older getlemen wearing a Hawian t-shirt and causal blue jeans. He introduced himself as the pastor with a friendly smile and firm handshake. We felt a bit over dressed but after attending the service we knew we had found our pastor and great place to worship God. Pastor Morris Barnett has been such an inspiring man in my life. His Sunday lesson is always rooted in the deep wisdom of the Bible. His charge to call each member to study the Bible has helped me to grow in my relationship with Jesus. His passionate voice drives me to a daily reading of the sacred scriptures. I must also admit that my devotion to read the Bible has created an intense appetite for spiritual well-being. I have come to hunger for any book that is written for the overall purpose of well-being and peace. I believe the hard work that spiritual men and women did before me was for me. Therefore, I hope to continue my practice of daily reading and deep study all the days of my life.

Prayer

Pray continually, give thanks in all circumstances:
for this is God's will for you in Christ Jesus.
—*1 Thess. 5:17–18 (NIV)*

Although reading and meditating have been priceless, prayer has been the amazing conduit of energy for me. Through a daily practice of prayer, I have been able to experience physical change in myself and the world around me. I would like to share three distinct types of daily prayer that you may find helpful in your personal journey.

1. *Gratitude Prayer:* This is my favorite type of prayer! I simply begin to list all of the things that I am grateful for (see self-inventory)—most importantly, how grateful I am for God's love. This allows us to remember what forces are really at play. I continue with almost every little thing that comes to mind—birds, trees, AC, heat, family, etc. I continue this process until I have completely run out of mental energy. I am convinced this mental purging helps your mind and body to align with the spirit of gratitude. To put it more aptly, I start my day with an Attitude of Gratitude.

2. *Forgiveness Prayer:* I like to view this prayer as my character refinement. I begin with an honest confession of my shortcomings. Just like in the gratitude prayer, I continue until I no longer can. This type of prayer, asking God to forgive my actions and mend my fractured character, helps acknowledge my imperfections daily. I must confront the desire in me that creates negative energy. Character is not easy to refine and needs attention daily.

Fun Fact: I fight with simple self-control daily, so I pray like this often.

3. *Intentional Prayer:* These are the prayers of my wants, needs, and hopes. I have learned that

I must be specific about the five *w's—who, what, when, where, and the how—*of my want. If I want a financial increase or a better job, then I first should determine how much, or what specific new job I want. If I hope for healing, I should be specific as to whom and what should be healed. For example, I might pray intentionally to heal the broken arm of a close friend instead of a general prayer of well-being. A true understanding of our wants and needs allows us to read what God's word says on the matter. If my wants, needs, or hopes are in accordance with God's principles, then they become available to me. These prayers require me to be patient and truly open to God's answers. Only when we are sure of what we want can God allow the universe to realign to our needs.

Meditate

Finally, brothers and sisters, whatever is true, whatever is noble, whatever is right, whatever is pure, whatever is lovely, whatever is admirable—if anything is excellent or praiseworthy—think about such things.
—Phil. 4:8 (NIV)

One of the most cherished skills in my recovery and spiritual growth has been a basic form of meditation and silence. A couple years after my injuries, I began to search for spiritual well-being from every dimension that was available to me. My daily practice up to that point consisted only of reading the Bible and prayer. Through my readings I became aware of God's direction toward practical meditation. As I started down the road of applying meditation, I discovered how extremely hard it was to obtain a reasonable level of inner silence. After I had acquired some basic skills around meditation, I was amazed by the impact it had on my daily life. My PTSD symptoms began to diminish. My days started with less anger and frustration. I noticed that I worried less about the small things in life. When I was in a crowded, hetic place, a simple breathing exercise and a directed awareness of God's love improved my current state within minutes. Because meditation seems to be when I am closest to God, I still work diligently at learning how to improve my inner silence each day. There are many different techniques and philosophies around the topic, but below I have added what has worked best for me. Please visit www.baptizedbyfire.com if your interested in additonal helpful tips or recommended readings on the topic of meditation.

Basic Body Check: Find a quiet place where you can settle and relax. Ground yourself with a chair or cushion or sit directly on the ground. Use a firm sitting posture but don't be tense. Begin to focus your attention on each individual breath that you take. Notice how the air flows into your nose, down into your lungs, and deep into your core. Try to avoid high chest breathing. This is when you only allow the air to flow into the chest but not deep into your diaphragm or core. Deep breaths that flow through the core allow for relaxation and peace. You can begin to guide your awareness to other parts of the body once you can easily inhale for four seconds and exhale for six seconds. Start by focusing on the top of the body at the head. Notice any signs of tightness, tension, or tingling. When any sign of the three *t's* appear, start to visualize clean air coming through your body and releasing the negative feelings. Continue to move down the body, noticing each connecting part. Spend as little or as much time as you need on each area of the body. Bring closure to your body check with an awareness of gratitude—a true and honest recognition of the mind and body that serves you each day. After my injury, this was the first method of meditation that I practiced. Now, I cannot image a day going by without spending at least ten minutes in silence.

> *God is far more interested in your char-*
> *acter than your comfort.*
> —*Pastor Morris Barnett, my pastor of Cliffdale*
> *Community Church, Fayetteville, North Carolina*

Through the practice of reading, prayer, and meditation, I truly learned to know God. Most importantly, I learned that knowing God is the surest way to knowing myself. God's law proved to define principles of the physical and spiritual universe that guided me to my true potential. Even the consequences of God's laws were designed to correct my course. I remember noticing the out-of-the-blue phone calls and e-mails from people whom I had been intentionally praying for, reporting significant increases in their well-being. Solutions to some of my difficult work situations began to unfold in the way I was intently praying. I began to meet amazing people who were profoundly grounded in God's love and grace. These experiences added more fuel to my own spiritual journey. But the true implication of my reactionary spirit was the vast emotional fulfillment from my wife and children. As a military man at heart, I could be mission driven and at times seem emotionally detached (the nice way of saying it). A new life of reading, daily prayer, and meditation rendered me open to the many blessings of my family's love. Some of those blessing appeared in my life as; family dinners, movie nights, family fun runs, and honest talk with my children. I was changed forever by the action of allowing God to dwell inside every part of my being.

When we redirect our time and energy that would normally be controlled by outside forces and fix ourselves to watch second by second with anticipation the wonders of God, we are then in our reactionary spirit. Only then can we begin to walk the path directed by God—free of fear and full of adventure.

Actions On

Read:

❖ "Do not think that I have come to abolish the Law or the Prophets: I have not come to abolish them but to fulfill them." —Matt. 5:17 (NIV)

❖ If you look for me wholeheartedly, you will find me. —Jer. 29:13 (NIV)

Pray:

Father, I accept you in my mind, body, and spirit. Please dwell inside every part of my being. Give me the discipline and courage to continue my practice of reading, praying, and meditation. It is by your love that I hope to live a life health, happiness, and fun.

Meditate:

Meditate on the following scripture:

Therefore if any man be in Christ, he is a new creature: old things are passed away; behold all things are become new.

—*2 Cor. 5:17 (NIV)*

Joe's Journal Points

1: What are my values that I cherish and strongly believe in?

2: Can I try to see it different today?

3: How can I react to my spirit today?

4: "What isn't moving for you?"

5: How might I use my personal beliefs, strengths and/or skills to improve upon a difficulty that I am dealing with?

6: Am I able to stand strong in accordance with my values?

7: What might I keep doing, start doing, and stop doing?

Reflective Reading

A kiss of the sun for pardon The song of the sun for mirth One is nearer God's heart in a garden Than anywhere else on earth.

—*Author Unknown*

four

Live a Proactive Life

(Reclaim myself in Christ)

As I mentioned earlier, I have spent the last three years sitting beside other combat veterans and listening to their deepest struggles. I have been immensely blessed with the opportunity to guide and inspire veterans away from the bondage of fear and toward a better way of living. This journey has been a constellation of painful tears, moments of despair, breakthroughs, closure, and pure joy. I have been humbled by these opportunities of vulnerability and have learned the true power of God's love. I have come to understand the blessing of proactive living. A life spent serving others, working diligently, and leading by example has become my True North. In stories to come, I want to highlight some of the novel blessings that follow a life of services, hard work, and leadership.

The Swift Kick

Ski Trip, Outdoor Combat Stress Retreat

The reward of serving others is unlike any other gift. Let me tell you a story about a warrior who I will call Sal.

Sal was a part of a group of warriors I took to the mountains for a combat stress retreat. They had all served in combat and wanted to learn skills that would help mitigate combat stress. Early on I noticed that Sal was physically present but seemed mentally detached from the group. He seem to shy away from the others and didn't seem to want to connect with anyone. After further investigation I learned that Sal was experiencing one of the lowest points of his life. His relationship with his wife had fallen apart, and his children were suffering in the struggle. Everything that he knew was slowly eroding away. His military career had abruptly ended, and now his family was to follow. Needless to say, he was running out of reasons to live. On the second day, Sal spoke up during one of our conversations. I cautiously prompted Sal with a concerned look. "You doing OK?" I asked. He dropped his head into his hands and replied, "I feel so damn alone. Every time I think I have this thing [PTSD] under control it delivers me A SWIFT KICK IN THE DICK!" Sal jumped up and threw his ski gloves across the table violently. "I LOST MY WIFE, KIDS, HOUSE, AND ALL MY FUCKING HOPE." He stared out the window for a spell. "Do you think this retreat will help me stop feeling so empty inside?" he asked.

I wanted to tell him that everything would be OK. I wanted to say that the world would stop kicking him in the nuts long enough for him to catch his breath. But the truth was, I wasn't certain what laid ahead. I did know that he would need to thoroughly mourn and take a good self-inventory. So I firmly replied, "I'm not certain if this retreat will help you, but we can approach today with everything we've got and see what happens." I showed compassion for Sal's mourning, and we took inventory over our few days together. Each day Sal fought for life in the snowy mountains of West Virginia. He spent time accepting the present experiences and allowed forgiveness into his heart. Each day working with Sal was spiritually replenishing. Watching him smile after a full day of skiing made all of the long nights sitting in group workshops seem petty in the whole scheme of things. Each night we would talk and discuss his future goals. I learned a lot from him that week—mostly that serving others is a revitalizing energy for one's self. Sal has continued to challenge himself and is fully aware of the benefits of serving others. He now is serving other wounded warriors on retreats such as deep-sea dives, sailing, overnight hikes, and many other adventurous excursions.

I have many stories like Sal's, great achievements of overcoming self-defeat and doubt. All of them have been profound confirmations of living a proactive life. Each warrior with whom I have come into contact with has left some personal influence on my soul. So much of my personal recovery and the power of helping others have led me to this point.

Following our reactionary spirit is only the start of aligning ourselves with our great design. We then must begin to take a step toward cultivating a proactive life of compassion and understanding. We can exercise this process by serving others, working hard, and leading by example. These purposeful actions can began to reveal true contentment in life.

> *Live a proactive life by serving others, working diligently, and lead by example.*
> —*Inspired by Pastor Morris Barnett*

Serve: Serving others brings joy to my soul. Nothing cures a prideful heart like selfless service to others. I have come to love serving others and find it to be a key purpose in life. I always get a bit choked up and feel truly blessed when I reflect on the hundreds of wounded veterans and family members I have helped along my journey. I only hope that whoever reads this book will know the power of service, too.

My mother always told me to be mindful of others. All the many years I watched her feed and care for our family with compassion and care. A heart of service was a mother's gift to an eager son. Thanks, Mom!

Work: My pastor preaches a strong message around the importance of diligent work. Each time I hear his message, I am always moved by the same words.

> *And whatever you do, whether in word or deed,*
> *do it all in the name of the Lord Jesus, giv-*
> *ing thanks to God the Father through him.*
> —Col. 3:17 (KJV)

Our gifts and talents should be exercised to our fullest potential. As a seasoned soldier, I can always find an enormous sense of gratitude in hard work, which is also a great way to foster self-gratitude and appreciation. Nothing feels better after a hard day of work than an exhausted body, a calm mind, and a quiet spirit.

My father was a Vietnam vet who insisted his children grow up knowing a day's work. A childhood of hard labor has set a path of diligent work. Thanks, Dad!

Lead: *Once a soldier, always a soldier.* The very first lesson I learned about army leadership was to lead by example and that this was the gold standard of leadership. Discipline and accountability are the qualities needed for this action. I find that leading by example is the best way to taste my own medicine. I cannot ask anyone to do something that I am not willing to do. I have also learned that I fail a lot at my own standards and practices. It is only by this action that I can set realistic goals and truly know my weak nature.

The army invested a lot of time retraining my shortcomings and building my leadership character. Thanks, Uncle Sam!

It is in this proactive living that I have come to peace with the search for meaning and purpose.

The man who is still looking for meaning is lost. Accepting God's will for us begins the journey of our limitless potential. God's will can unlock the deepest power in us all.

Be the change you want to see in the world.
—*Mahatma Gandhi*

Actions On

Read:

❖ Whatever you do, work at it with all your heart, as working for the Lord, not for human masters, since you know that you will receive an inheritance from the Lord as a reward. It is the Lord Christ you are serving. —Col. 3:23–24 (NIV)

Pray:

Father, help me live a proactive life for your glory. Help me cultivate the heart to serve, the strength to work, and the courage to lead. It is under your design that I hope to find rest in your love.

Meditate:

Meditate on the following scripture:

> *You, my brothers and sisters, were called to be free. But do not use your freedom to indulge the flesh; rather, serve one another humbly in love.*
> —*Gal. 5:13(NIV)*

Joe's Journal Points

1: Today I will be brave and just *try...*

2: Can I set a goal that I am willing to commit energy and action to?

3: Today you can expect from me...

4: How can I make it better?

5: Can I accept my effort today?

6: *The pessimist looks at opportunities and sees difficulties. The optimist looks at difficulties and see opportunities. —Author Unknown*

7: When my challenge appears today, I will...

Reflection Reading

The supreme prayer of my heart is not be rich, famous, powerful, or too good, but to be radiant. I desire to radiate health, calm courage, cheerfulness and good will. I wish to live without hate, whim, jealousy, envy or fear. I wish to be simple, honest, frank, natural, clean in mind and clean in body, unaffected, ready to say "I do not know." If so it be, to meet all men on an absolute equality, to face any obstacle and meet every difficulty unabashed and unafraid. I wish others to live their lives, too, up to their fullest and best. To that end I pray that I may never meddle, interfere, dictate, give advice that is not wanted, or assist when my services are not needed. If I can help people I will do it, by giving them a chance to help themselves; and I can uplift or inspire, let it be by example, inference,

suggestion, rather than by injunction and dictation.
That is to say, I desire to be radiant, to radiate life.
—*Prayer found near Tours, France, in 1918,*
by AEF Doughboy of World War I

Epilogue:

Embrace the Challenge

We have finally arrived at the last part of this book. All of the insights gained through these experiences are priceless to me, no matter how painful or tough they might have been. Self-acceptance and forgiveness were deep personal victories along my journey. Those victories led me to a practical understanding of my spirit and the true power of proactive living. I am committed to living out the rest of my days guiding and inspiring others along this great adventure.

Note: You can embrace the challenge at *www. Baptizedbyfire.com*

I challenge anyone who is in pain or unsure of their true nature and purpose to commit to a small, twenty-eight-day challenge. This book is separated into four chapters that all end with some practical applications. Examine each one separately over the next four weeks. Commit to one hour each day reviewing the *Actions On* and *Joe's Journal Points*. Take a deeper study into the scriptures and personal insights. I suggest taking this book to a place that is fairly peaceful and free of distractions. Start with the body scan (see chapter 3) to settle the mind and body and become more aware and present. Then review the *Actions On* exercises. There are seven reflection questions in the *Joe's Journal Points* section. Choose one for each day to reflect on and write about. Journal entries do not need to be long essays that are up for review by some old crusty college professor. They can serve as short reminders of thoughts, feelings, or actions that may have surfaced during a reflection.

Note: I find journaling to be extremely helpful in keeping my thoughts and actions focused on what is most important to me.

I am confident that a sense of peace will consume the soul if an honest and consistent effort is made throughout the twenty-eight days. I hope that I have made a sufficient case to provide hope, even if it is for just one person. I pray that no one comes to learn these points the way I did. I do not regret the burns, disfigurement, and scars that I have gained along the journey. My only regrets are my past actions that may have hurt someone and the time I have wasted because of my ignorance about these insights.

May our days be blessed with God's love and a life of meaningful adventure. Amen.

Appendix 1

Goal Setting with SMART

- *Specific:* "What do I want to achieve?"
- *Measure:* "What are my main measures for this achievement? In other words, what will I see, hear, or feel when I have achieved the above?"
- *Attainable:* "Is achieving my goal within my control?"
- *Realistic:* "Is my goal realistically connected to the overall health and well-being of my mind, body, or spirit?"
- *Time:* "When will I complete my goal?"

Appendix 2

Joe's Personal Mission Statement

I have come to realize that I know nothing about anything outside these few truths:

- Learn to love God first before anything else.
- Always align your mind and body with your spirit.
- All people matter.
- Always express humility, forgiveness, and gratitude in your presence.
- Spend all your time in the service of others.
- Courage is the antidote to fear.

These values have been forged under the suffering of my many failures and loss battles. Through those experiences, a love for God, self, family, and humanity have emerged.

Appendix 3

Additional Journal Points and Reflections

1. *I believe that no man can be completely able to summon all his strength, all his will, all his energy, for that last desperate move, till he is convinced the last bridge is down behind him and that there is nowhere to go but on. —Heinrich Harrer*

2. *To venture causes anxiety, but not to venture is to lose one's self. And to venture in the highest sense is precisely to become conscious of one's self. —Soren Kierkegaard*

3. *In the depth of winter, I finally learned that within me there lay an invincible summer. — Albert Camus*

4. *You've got to leave before you can arrive. — Author Unknown*

5. *The mark of a great fighter is how he acts when he's getting licked. —Sugar Ray Robinson*

6. *I've endured many hardships to test my determination. I went without food for many days. I refused to lie down to sleep for many nights. Endurance became the food to nourish my heart and diligence the pillow to rest my head. It is important to patiently endure the inevitable hardships of our simple existence without being lazy or disgruntled. Let love and compassion be your ready response to every situation. —Mae Chee Kaew 1901–1991, Thai Buddhist nun*

7. *I believe that courage is all too often mistakenly seen as the absence of fear. If you descend by a rope from a cliff and are not fearful to some degree, you are either crazy or unaware. Courage is seeing your fear, in a realistic perspective, defining it, considering alternatives and choosing to function in spite of risks. — Leonard Zunin, The First Four Minutes*